This Edition © Copyright 1994 Omnibus Press
(A Division of Book Sales Limited)

Edited by Chris Charlesworth
Cover & book designed by Graham Sturt, 4i Limited
Picture research by David Brolan

ISBN: 0.7119.4164.5
Order No: OP47652

All rights reserved. No part of this book may be reproduced in any form or by any electronic or mechanical means, including information storage or retrieval systems, without permission in writing from the publisher, except by a reviewer who may quote brief passages.

Exclusive Distributors
Book Sales Limited,
8/9 Frith Street,
London W1V 5TZ, UK.

Music Sales Corporation,
257 Park Avenue South,
New York, NY10010, USA.

Music Sales Pty Limited,
Lisgar House, 30-32 Carrington Street,
Sydney, NSW2000, Australia.

To the Music Trade only:
Music Sales Limited,
8/9, Frith Street,
London W1V 5TZ, UK.

Picture credits: All pictures courtesy of Lloyd Barclay

Every effort has been made to trace the copyright holders of the photographs in this book but one or two were unreachable. We would be grateful if the photographers concerned would contact us.

Printed by Ebenezer Baylis & Son Limited, Worcester.

A catalogue record for this book is available from the British Library.

OMNIBUS PRESS

Metallica

Pizza-faced complexions, bum-fluff stubble, hair by Duckhams and the sartorial sophistication of doorway dossers, the young Metallica that made their name at the Old Waldorf club in downtown San Francisco were hardly the kind of kids you could imagine graduating to the Lear jet-and-limo league of multi-platinum privilege.

But that was back in 1982, just before metal's New Wave crashed foaming like a Bondi breaker, leaving in its wake a blood-curdling clutch of off-shoots. Thrash Metal was the most popular of these supersonic subdivisions, and Metallica's 1983 début album 'Kill 'Em All' arguably its first stepping stone to notoriety. The dense

before persuading the local Metal Blade label to include their song 'Hit The Lights' on the influential 'Metal Massacre I' compilation album. But it was when Grant was replaced by Dave Mustaine that the fireworks really began to fly, as a clash of egos between the fiery new guitarist and his counterpart Hetfield fanned the flames within an already explosive outfit.

Early shows around the predominantly glam-based territory of LA included a date with Yorkshire warriors Saxon at the Whiskey-A-Go-Go in March '82 and whatever support slots they could blag at dives like The Roxy, The Troubadour and The Starwood. A typical set would be moulded around a core of New Wave Of British Heavy Metal covers, such as Savage's 'Buried Alive' and 'Let It Loose', Sweet Savage's 'Killing Time' and Blitzkrieg's eponymous break-neck anthem, plus any number of songs from Lars'

Pizza-faced complexions, bum-fluff stubble, hair by Duckhams and the sartorial sophistication of doorway dossers, the young Metallica that made their name at the Old Waldorf club in downtown San Francisco were hardly the kind of kids you could imagine graduating to the Lear jet-and-limo league of multi-platinum privilege.

underground following that the band had nurtured with their 'No Life Til Leather' demo around 1981/82 was instantly mobilised, and as the Thrash craze swept across the face of rock'n'roll like a nasty rash, Metallica were squeezed to the forefront and hailed as heroes.

By the time 'Kill 'Em All' put Thrash on the map, Metallica had crystallised into the four-man line-up of James Hetfield (rhythm guitar/vocals), Lars Ulrich (drums), Cliff Burton (bass) and Kirk Hammett (lead guitar). The band was originally the brainchild of Danish-born Ulrich and LA-local Hetfield, who'd scouted around the garages of Smog City to find a guitarist called Lloyd Grant and a bassist by the name of Ron McGovney,

favourites, Diamond Head. While a seething mass of influences from Black Sabbath to The Ramones and Motorhead to Discharge would come boiling to the surface like a cocktail of impurities during the band's own convulsive compositions.

Few of those fortunate enough to have witnessed these formative forays into the glare of the spotlight (well, the murk of the odd 40 watt bulb, at least) would claim that the band were anything other than a steamroller on steroids, awash with a heady mixture of testosterone and Biactol. But the more astute observers confessed to a gut-feeling which told them there was more to this eight-legged earache than the white noise blur of Thrash's faster-than-thou dogmatism. And

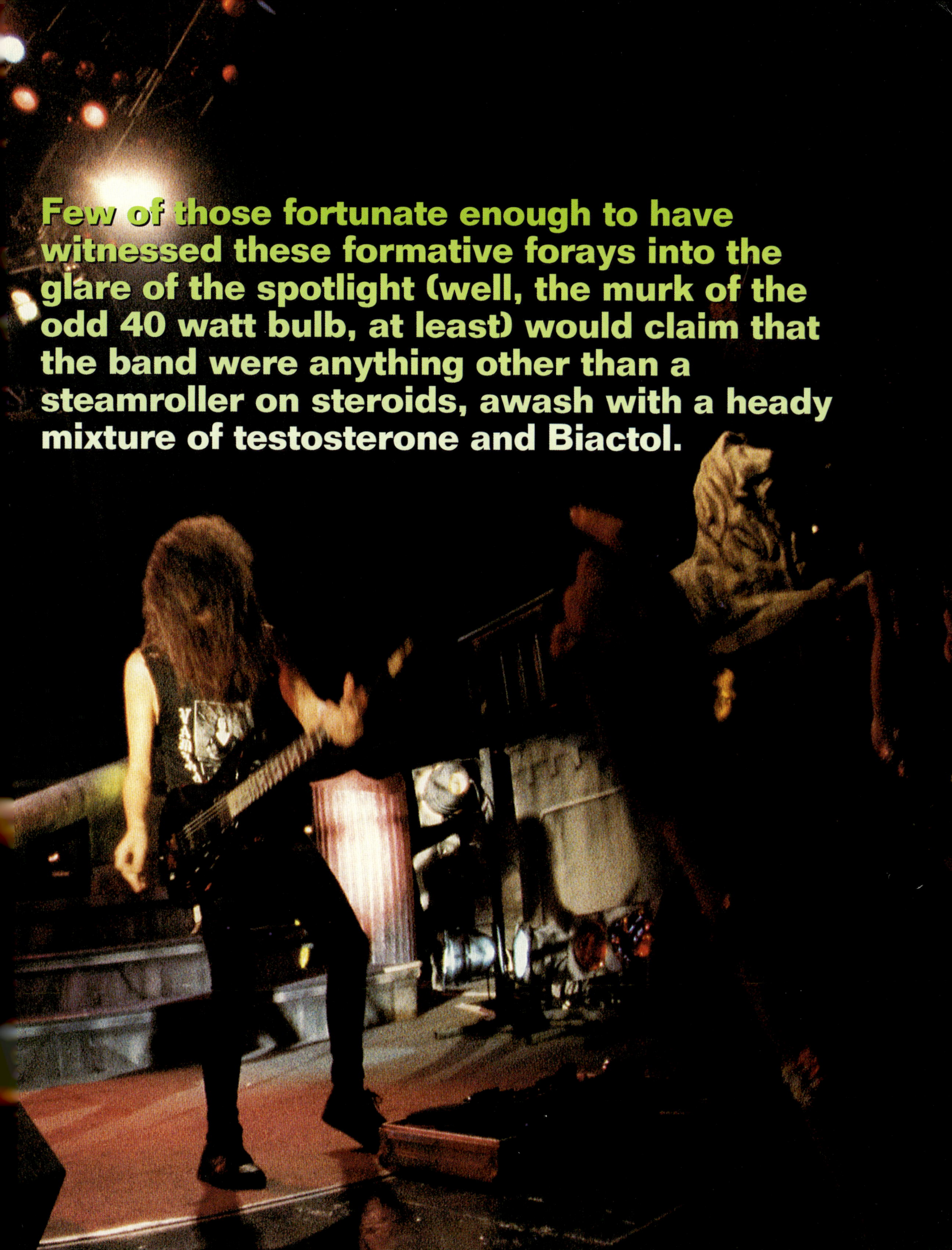

Few of those fortunate enough to have witnessed these formative forays into the glare of the spotlight (well, the murk of the odd 40 watt bulb, at least) would claim that the band were anything other than a steamroller on steroids, awash with a heady mixture of testosterone and Biactol.

the onstage friction between Hetfield and Mustaine, both battling for glory, always ensured that the shows were knife-edge affairs of entertaining unpredictability.

Not that the pink-lurex-and-lipstick brigade of LA's dominant glam scene took to these snivelling shits who seemed to be ingesting metal yet puking up punk. Indeed, during 1982 the band decided to leave the sleaze of Sunset Strip to the likes of Mötley Crüe and Ratt and relocate up the coast to San Francisco, where Thrash was held in far greater esteem, most notably by a large network of 'underground' fans who called themselves the Bay Area 'Bangers.

Metallica secured shows at The Stone and, around October time, at the Old Waldorf, which held a weekly showcase for local rock talent known as 'Metal Monday'. Despite usually occupying the middle spot on a three-band bill, their rocketing popularity often meant they'd steal the headliners' thunder, and word of their conquests soon reached Europe, where the 'No Life Til Leather' demo was much sought-after.

Speed was Metallica's business, and business was good. In amongst their rubber-burning repertoire were titles like 'Metal Militia', 'Phantom Lord', 'Jump In The Fire', 'The Mechanix' and 'No Remorse', and there certainly wasn't any remorse

Jersey entrepreneur Johnny Zazula. He would, of course, return to the fray with a new band called Megadeth, but for the time being at least Metallica were relieved to see the back of him.

Mustaine's replacement was Kirk Hammett, from San Francisco Speed Metal specialists Exodus. He made his live début with Metallica at the Showplace in New Jersey during April '83 and exorcised the ghost of Mustaine in a hail of fiendishly frenzied solos when the band's début album 'Kill 'Em All' appeared in July. It was apparent to most people that while Hammett may have lacked the sheer force of personality of his temperamental predecessor, his fast-forward style of guitar playing and easy-going demeanour made for a better balance within the ranks, and his appointment seemed to lessen the chance of internal combustion.

Johnny Zazula, who now not only managed the band but also ran the record company, Megaforce, which financed 'Kill 'Em All', capitalised on the buzz the record had created by sending the band on a 36-date US tour with Tyneside trio (and Megaforce labelmates) Raven. The venture sprawled throughout the summer and screamed to a halt at The Stone in San Francisco, where Metallica's status had been further enhanced by the recruitment of local lads Burton and Hammett.

> **Speed was Metallica's business, and business was good. In amongst their rubber-burning repertoire were titles like 'Metal Militia', 'Phantom Lord', 'Jump In The Fire', 'The Mechanix' and 'No Remorse', and there certainly wasn't any remorse in the way they battered their audiences into submission. In terms of tempo, Metallica were faster than a hippo on skis, and twice as heavy.**

in the way they battered their audiences into submission. In terms of tempo, Metallica were faster than a hippo on skis, and twice as heavy.

Continuing grief within the band, however, soon precipitated a change in personnel. Ron McGovney was replaced by Cliff Burton from Frisco outfit Trauma and, several months later, Dave Mustaine was finally fired, thanks largely to his self-destructive dalliance with booze and 'chemical entertainment products'. His last show with Metallica was in New York on a bill that also featured Venom and Vandenburg, shortly after the band had been lured to the East Coast by New

Further shows in the US followed throughout the rest of '83, before Metallica made their first live appearance on foreign soil at the Volkshaus in Zurich, Switzerland, on February 3, 1984. They'd been booked to open for Black Metal buffoons Venom on the so-called 'Seven Dates Of Hell' tour (in reality six European shows, plus a Hammersmith Odeon gig some nine months later, which didn't involve Metallica!), and while the undertaking was one of mixed fortunes, most people agreed Metallica had the edge over Cronos and Co.

The highlight of the tour was the Aardschok

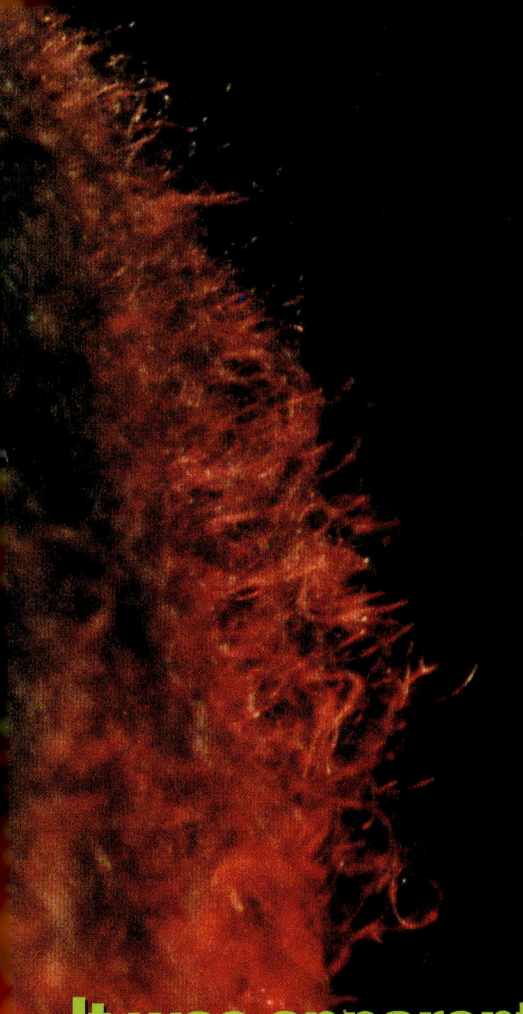

Festival at Ijsselhal in Zwolle, Holland, on February 11. Metallica marched on stage to the Spaghetti Western strains of an Ennio Morricone intro tape, before slam-diving headlong into 'Hit The Lights', followed by 'The Four Horsemen', 'Jump In The Fire', 'Phantom Lord', 'Motorbreath' and 'Whiplash', each song shunting into the rear of the previous blow-out like juggernauts in a fog-bound motorway pile-up. It was a frantic performance, punctuated only by Cliff Burton's peculiar bass solo spot, dubbed 'Pulling Teeth', in which he of the rabid Rickenbacker and bell-bottomed jeans demonstrated his unique 'helicopter' headbanging technique, whipping his lank locks around in Anadin-inducing rotation.

Burton's surreal solo and general onstage dementia was quickly established as an essential component of any Metallica show. His freakish, improvisational style added a degree of spontaneity to the band's stage routine which set them apart from many of their cack-handed contemporaries, and his gonzoid delivery made him a firm favourite with the fans (of which there were 6,000 at Aardschok).

Metallica's 90-minute set at the festival was completed by a new song, 'Ride The Lightning', and an old gem, 'Metal Militia'. The unveiling of the new track was of special significance, as it turned

the Breaking Wind (né Sound) Festival in Paris, and then rejoined Raven for a show at the Roseland Ballroom in New York. The year was rounded off with another, more prolonged stint in Europe, finishing up at the Lyceum in London five days before Christmas.

New management (Q Prime) and a new US record company (Elektra) helped pave the way for Metallica to take another step up the ladder in late '84, while an American tour with close friends Armored Saint in February/March '85 served to further incite a groundswell of support. But perhaps the most crucial breakthrough of 1985 came at Castle Donington in August, where the band rubbed shoulders with a host of highly unsuitable bedfellows (ZZ Top, Marillion, Bon Jovi, Ratt and Magnum) and yet won widespread praise for a performance of chilling intensity. Thrash had arrived on the big stage, and as if to confirm this notion to their fellow Americans, Metallica lined up alongside The Scorpions, Ratt, Y&T, Rising Force and Victory for Bill Graham's massive Day On The Green festival in San Francisco a fortnight later.

With the release of the band's third album, 'Master Of Puppets', which spewed from the womb in January 1987, came confirmation that Metallica's amazing progress was more than just

It was apparent to most people that while Hammett may have lacked the sheer force of personality of his temperamental predecessor, his fast-forward style of guitar playing and easy-going demeanour made for a better balance within the ranks, and his appointment seemed to lessen the chance of internal combustion.

out to be the title cut from Metallica's second album, which was eventually released in the UK on the Music For Nations label in July 1984. Those who attended the band's first UK show, at London's Marquee on March 27, also got to hear 'Ride The Lightning', plus three other new songs destined for the album: 'For Whom The Bell Tolls', 'Fight Fire With Fire' and 'Creeping Death'.

Another show at the Marquee followed on April 8, and then in June the band returned to the Continent to open up for every Avon Lady's nightmare, Twisted Sister. The rest of the year was spent straddling the Atlantic, as Metallica appeared as The Four Horsemen at a 'secret' gig at Mabuhay Gardens in San Francisco during late June, bounded back to Europe in late August for

a figment of the metal media's imagination. 'Master Of Puppets' entered the UK charts at No.41, and also breached the Top 30 Stateside, a clear indication that Metallica were in the process of transcending the blinkered Thrash genre.

Yet another invaluable leg-up at this juncture came from Ozzy Osbourne, who hired the young guns for his extensive US tour from March to August. Christened the 'Damage Inc.' tour it took Metallica out of the clubs and established them as an arena act with superbowl pretensions. Indeed, the only damage incurred on the trip was a broken bone in James Hetfield's left wrist (the skateboard strikes again), which allowed guitar roadie Jim Marshall a moment or two of glory, keeping up with the rampant rhythms while

Indeed, the only damage incurred on the trip was a broken bone in James Hetfield's left wrist (the skateboard strikes again), which allowed guitar roadie Jim Marshall a moment or two of glory, keeping up with the rampant rhythms while Hetfield concentrated on perfecting his bear-with-sore-bollocks vocal style.

Hetfield concentrated on perfecting his bear-with-sore-bollocks vocal style.

Marshall remained in the band for a highly acclaimed European tour with old pals Anthrax during September, but the intention was always that the line-up would revert to a four-piece as soon as Hetfield had recovered. Sadly, a tragedy on an icy road in Denmark would mean that that four-piece would not include Cliff Burton.

Unwittingly, British fans paid their last respects to 24-year-old Cliff Burton when he performed his infamous bass solo at Hammersmith Odeon on September 21. Metallica left London for Scandinavia the following day and fulfilled live commitments in Lund, Oslo and Stockholm, before travelling through the night of Friday September 26 to Copenhagen. At 5.15am (UK time) on the Saturday the tour bus crashed into a ditch just outside the small Danish town of Ljungby, and Burton was crushed to death in the wreckage. Many original fans of the band maintain that the true spirit of Metallica died with him.

Shaken but not deterred, Metallica immediately bounced back with new bassist Jason Newsted, from the Phoenix-based Flotsam And Jetsam. He made his live début with Hetfield, Ulrich and Hammett at Shibuya Kokaido in Tokyo, Japan, on November 15, and while it was clear that in terms of character he was more Cliff Richard than Cliff Burton, Newsted worked hard to ingrain himself in the fabric of Metallica.

An eventful year ended with more shows in America in the company of Metal Church, and the New Year began with Newsted making his début in Europe,

Burton's surreal solo and general onstage dementia was quickly established as an essential component of any Metallica show. His freakish, improvisational style added a degree of spontaneity to the band's stage routine which set them apart from many of their cack-handed contemporaries, and his gonzoid delivery made him a firm favourite with the fans.

metalli

calive!

Shaken but not deterred, Metallica immediately bounced back with new bassist Jason Newsted, from the Phoenix-based Flotsam And Jetsam. He made his live début with Hetfield, Ulrich and Hammett at Shibuya Kokaido in Tokyo, Japan, on November 15, and while it was clear that in terms of character he was more Cliff Richard than Cliff Burton, Newsted worked hard to ingrain himself in the fabric of Metallica.

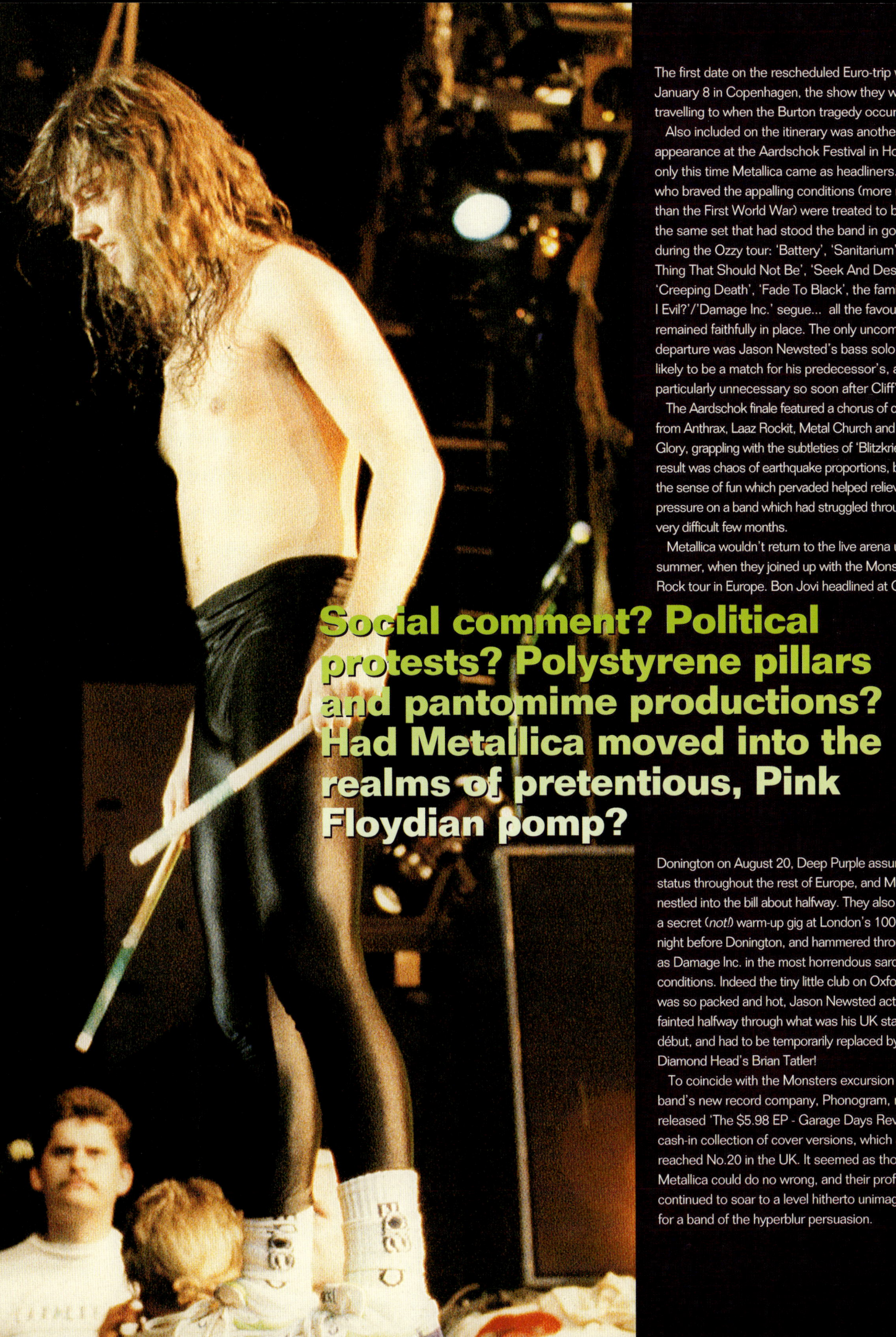

The first date on the rescheduled Euro-trip was on January 8 in Copenhagen, the show they were travelling to when the Burton tragedy occured.

Also included on the itinerary was another appearance at the Aardschok Festival in Holland, only this time Metallica came as headliners. Those who braved the appalling conditions (more mud than the First World War) were treated to basically the same set that had stood the band in good stead during the Ozzy tour: 'Battery', 'Sanitarium', 'The Thing That Should Not Be', 'Seek And Destroy', 'Creeping Death', 'Fade To Black', the familiar 'Am I Evil?'/'Damage Inc.' segue... all the favourites remained faithfully in place. The only uncomfortable departure was Jason Newsted's bass solo, never likely to be a match for his predecessor's, and particularly unnecessary so soon after Cliff's death.

The Aardschok finale featured a chorus of cronies from Anthrax, Laaz Rockit, Metal Church and Crimson Glory, grappling with the subtleties of 'Blitzkrieg'. The result was chaos of earthquake proportions, but then the sense of fun which pervaded helped relieve the pressure on a band which had struggled through a very difficult few months.

Metallica wouldn't return to the live arena until the summer, when they joined up with the Monsters Of Rock tour in Europe. Bon Jovi headlined at Castle

Social comment? Political protests? Polystyrene pillars and pantomime productions? Had Metallica moved into the realms of pretentious, Pink Floydian pomp?

Donington on August 20, Deep Purple assumed that status throughout the rest of Europe, and Metallica nestled into the bill about halfway. They also threw in a secret (*not!*) warm-up gig at London's 100 Club the night before Donington, and hammered through a set as Damage Inc. in the most horrendous sardine conditions. Indeed the tiny little club on Oxford Street was so packed and hot, Jason Newsted actually fainted halfway through what was his UK stage début, and had to be temporarily replaced by Diamond Head's Brian Tatler!

To coincide with the Monsters excursion the band's new record company, Phonogram, rush-released 'The $5.98 EP - Garage Days Revisited', a cash-in collection of cover versions, which actually reached No.20 in the UK. It seemed as though Metallica could do no wrong, and their profile continued to soar to a level hitherto unimaginable for a band of the hyperblur persuasion.

The only danger in all this was the risk of overkill, and so it was that the band spent far longer than usual working on their fourth album, '...And Justice For All'. The record was finally released on September 8 1988, by which time Metallica had just completed their commitments on an American version of the Monsters Of Rock tour. Headlined by Van Halen and also featuring The Scorpions, Dokken and Led Zep-clones Kingdom Come, the tour ran from May to July but suffered from poor ticket sales during a period when concert attendances were well down on the norm in America. Yet Metallica escaped from the commercial flop with their reputation intact, and the hysterical reception afforded to the new album confirmed this. It gatecrashed the UK charts the week after its release and stormed to No.4.

After warming up with another 'secret' show at one of their old haunts, The Troubadour in Hollywood – this time under the monicker Frayed Ends – Metallica flew to Britain to begin what was to become known as the 'Damaged Justice' tour. The first date was Edinburgh Playhouse on

in a violent burst of wanton vandalism, and fans were left with the task of drawing their own conclusions as to the message that the band were aiming to put across.

Social comment? Political protests? Polystyrene pillars and pantomime productions? Had Metallica moved into the realms of pretentious, Pink Floydian pomp?

Nah, it was simply an attempt at doing something different, not to be taken too seriously. The new live show ran to two-and-a-half hours and more, with some encore segments stretching to eight numbers (including, on one or two occasions, a version of Iron Maiden's 'Prowler'), and the distraction of the new stage set helped give the show a slightly more interesting dimension without detracting too much from the music.

The 'Damaged Justice' tour worked its way through Europe during November and then switched to America, where Metallica finished the year on a high with a string of sell-out dates at the prestigious Long Beach Arena in LA. After the Christmas break the excursion continued to blaze

And while there was still some substance to the argument that the various solo sections were an unnecessary indulgence – this was Metallica after all, not ELP! – it did appear that The Four Hoarse Men had tightened up their act.

Perhaps, after over 300 shows in the two years since August '91, Metallica were getting the hang of this playing live business!

September 24, whereafter the band covered most of the main cities in the British Isles and Ireland, rounding things off with three manic nights at Hammersmith Odeon in October.

The 'Damaged Justice' tour was in fact a significant progression in terms of Metallica's live show. Previously their stage presentation had been basic to say the least, but now with more funds at their disposal they could aim for something more ambitious, and so it was that the '...Justice...' concept was transformed into a visual extravaganza that took everyone by surprise.

The new stage set was constructed to reflect the artwork on the album cover, complete with a huge monolith of Blind Lady Justice, which was gradually erected throughout the show by a clever system of pulleys and wires. At the climax of '...And Justice For All' the statue was destroyed

a trail across the States until May, whereupon Metallica headed Down Under for shows in Australia (their first), New Zealand (ditto) and Japan. It was at these concerts that the band's management introduced the idea of 'legal bootlegging' – cordoning off an area behind the sound desk and allowing those fans prepared to purchase a special ticket for the enclosure to tape the show. It was an idea that had worked for the Grateful Dead in America, and needless to say it proved immensely popular with Metallifans, who'd formed an extensive network of tape-trading in any case.

The summer saw Metallica back in the USA, October brought visits to Brazil and Argentina and by the end of 1989 Metallica could lay claim to have performed over 250 shows on the 'Damaged Justice' tour. Once again a long break

as required in order to recharge severely run-down batteries, and Metallica wouldn't perform live again until May 1990, when they breezed through Germany, France and Holland, stopping off in Britain for three shows in London (Wembley Arena), Birmingham (NEC) and Glasgow (SECC), plus an unannounced appearance with Metal Church at the Marquee on May 11.

Inevitably, Phonogram seized on the opportunity to release yet more 'collector's item' product, and hence 'The Good, The Bad & The Live: The Six And A Half Anniversary 12" Collection' was shoved into the shops a bit sharpish – a box set of all Metallica's EPs to date, plus three previously unavailable live recordings. By this stage the band were having trouble justifying the record company's blatant squeeze-it-dry philosophy, but the demand for anything with the Metallica name stamped across it – T-shirts, videos, magazines, etc. – remained unfeasibly strong.

Two shows in Canada supporting Aerosmith was all that stood between Metallica and a long stint in the recording studio during the summer of 1990, a

Metallica returned home to California in October to commence a mammoth tour of the States – seven months solid, with just one show at the Tokyo Dome in Japan on New Year's Eve 1991 to break the routine. As if to confirm that they really were in the supergroup bracket now, the band unveiled an elaborate new stage show which found them performing 'in the round' – in the middle of the arena on a diamond-shaped stage, with the fans seated all the way around. The idea had been used by rock giants such as Yes in the '70s and Def Leppard in the '80s, only Metallica added an innovation to the concept by introducing a special enclosure in the middle of the stage (known as the 'snakepit') reserved for around 120 fortunate fans – competition winners, for example – who would enjoy the unique privilege of a 'roadie's eye' view of the action.

The new stage production meant no-one in the band could hide, and the onus was on James in particular to involve all the fans in the 360 degree set-up. For that purpose a dozen microphones were positioned around the stage, allowing him to roam freely, while the ever-hyper Lars also insisted on a

summer, a prospect made all the more intriguing by the inclusion of fellow Frisco freaks Faith No More as bill-openers.

No sooner had it started, however, than the tour ran into problems (par for the course in the wacky world of Gn'R). James Hetfield suffered second degree burns on his hand after a close encounter with a flashbomb in Montreal during early August (an incident which inevitably curtailed the band's set and later led to some shows being cancelled), while the same night Axl Rose incited a riot by walking off stage long before the scheduled end of the Guns show.

Amazingly, the tour also began to experience poor ticket sales, an indication that the much-mentioned recession had hit America as well as Europe. Indeed, the liaison with Guns didn't last as long as was originally intended, and Metallica headed off on their own on what was commonly being referred to as the 'Wherever I May Roam' tour.

Mid-October found Metallica back in Europe, kicking off with an appearance in Ghent, Belgium, before thundering into the UK to lay waste to Wembley Arena (two nights), the SECC in

And so, in the late summer of '93, the mighty Metallica machine finally shuddered to a standstill, leaving behind a mass of memories as vivid as the music itself.

stint that would in fact cost the band over $1 million. The long awaited and self-titled fifth album wouldn't see daylight until August 1991, some three years after '...And Justice For All', but when it finally emerged – premièred at two special 'listening parties', one at Madison Square Garden in New York, the other at Hammersmith Odeon in London – any fears that the band's snowballing career might have lost some momentum in the long lay-off were immediately dispelled. Some six million sales later (the record entered the US charts at No.1), even their most fervent critics had to concede that, like some chronic disease, Metallica were here to stay.

To promote the new album and single (the extraordinarily successful 'Enter Sandman'), Metallica joined the European Monsters Of Rock bill for the third time in six years, where they played a supporting role to AC/DC. Also on the menu for the cruise around the Continent were Mötley Crüe, Queensryche and The Black Crowes, and for the first time the Monsters made it to Russia, with a show at the Tushino airfield near Moscow on September 28. Without the pressure of headlining Metallica could relax and simply enjoy themselves on the tour, and most of those who caught the show agreed that it was a far better experience than the '87 version.

After 20 Monsters gigs in 18 European cities,

greater degree of mobility, sitting astride a drum kit which slid up and down the stage on tracks.

Another departure was that no support band was booked for the tour. Instead, the fans were warmed up by a half-hour video which recalled the highlights of Metallica's career to date. Once again it was an interesting idea, but it did suggest to some critics that Metallica were taking themselves too seriously, and that the whole package was rather too self-congratulatory for comfort.

Nevertheless, the success of the tour was never in doubt and Metallica continued to set the standards which most of their gutter-buddies from the Thrash brotherhood could only dream about. They could now line up alongside some of the biggest names in contemporary popular music – Elton John, David Bowie, George Michael – for a show like the Freddie Mercury Concert For AIDS Awareness at Wembley Stadium on April 20 1992, without being overawed. To all intents and purposes, Metallica were now part of the establishment, an incredible achievement for a bunch of oiks who hardly had two chords to rub together when they started.

Indeed, the only rock band to come close to Metallica in terms of current record sales in 1992 was Guns n' Roses, so it was perhaps fitting that the two giants should link up for a tour of America during the

Glasgow, Whitley Bay Ice Rink, The Point in Dublin, Sheffield Arena, Manchester's G-Mex and Birmingham's NEC (two nights). The rest of November and December was spent zig-zagging across mainland Europe, from Holland to Helsinki and from Barcelona to Berlin, and the whole circus came grinding to a halt at the Globen in Stockholm on December 18.

Just over a month later the wheels turned again, and January and February saw another 20 shows in the US and Canada. Five nights at the Sports Palace in Mexico City took Metallica into March and then the Air Miles really began to build up as the band notched up visits to Hawaii, Japan, New Zealand, Australia, Indonesia, Singapore, Thailand, the Philippines, Brazil, Chile and Argentina in a gruelling ten week spell.

Many of these territories still remain largely untouched by the hand of Western rock bands, so in places like Singapore and the Philippines Metallica were undoubtedly venturing into the unknown. Yet the only major blot on the landscape was a riot at the Lebak Bulus Stadium in Jakarta, Indonesia, where some 5,000 ticket-less fans went on the rampage outside the venue, burning cars and smashing windows. The promoter, who'd grossly overpriced the tickets in the first place, had no option but to open the doors of the stadium and let the disgruntled

punters in for free.

By May 19 Metallica were back in Europe, kicking off yet another leg of what might have been called the 'Centipede Tour' with a show in Hanover, Germany. For the next six weeks the band took in most of the Continent, including some of the more unusual locations such as Istanbul, Athens and Tel Aviv, playing mostly outdoor shows and festivals.

The band's only UK appearance of the summer came on June 5 in front of 60,000 fans at the Milton Keynes Bowl, where they were supported by Dave Mustaine's Megadeth, Jock rockers The Almighty and the newly reformed Diamond Head (who, incidentally, opened their set with 'Am I Evil?').

The new Metallica set featured one or two changes from the one which had been flogged to death across America for the best part of the last two years, with an emphasis placed on older material. 'Disposable Heroes' and 'The Thing That Should Not Be' from the 'Master Of Puppets' album were re-introduced, plus 'The Four Horsemen' from 'Kill 'Em All' and the slightly more obscure 'So What', which had only previously been used as a B-side.

The backbone of the show retained its familiarity, however, and those who craved the usual helping of 'Creeping Death', 'To Live Is To Die', 'Master Of Puppets', 'Seek And Destroy', 'Sad But True' and 'Battery' were not disappointed.

Also in the two-and-half-hour set was a brutal cover of The Misfits' 'Last Caress', a storming 'So What' and a poignant rendition of 'Orion', the instrumental which Cliff Burton made his own. And while there was still some substance to the argument that the various solo sections were an unnecessary indulgence – this was Metallica after all, not ELP! – it did appear that The Four Hoarse Men had tightened up their act.

Perhaps, after over 300 shows in the two years since August '91, Metallica were getting the hang of this playing live business!

And so, in the late summer of '93, the mighty Metallica machine finally shuddered to a standstill, leaving behind a mass of memories as vivid as the music itself. The walrus-moustachioed Hetfield, hunched over his mikestand and thrashing the crap out of his guitar in a blur of silver skull-rings. The newly cropped Jason Newsted, all psycho-stares and stomping arrogance, cavorting around the stage like a refugee from Sham 69. Little Kirk Hammett, legs like After Eights, hair like a King Charles Spaniel, running his fingers up the down the neck of his guitar with the ferocity of a sewing machine. And last but not least (if he has anything to do with it), Great Dane Lars Ulrich, pummelling his wall of drums like a pocket-sized Viking... in between posing for photographs, of course! Smile please...

Further reading: 'Metallica - A Visual Documentary' by Mark Putterford and Xavier Russell (Omnibus Press).

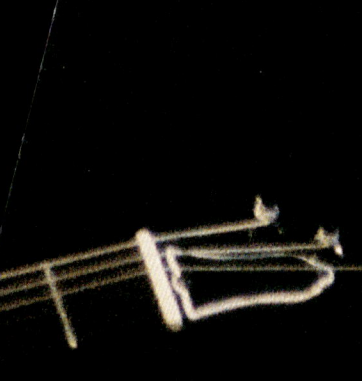

METALLICA DISCOGRAPHY

UK SINGLES

Jump In The Fire/ Seek And Destroy (live)/ Phantom Lord (live)
(also available in red vinyl edition)
Music For Nations 12KUT 105
January 1984

Reissued as a shaped picture disc
Music For Nations PKUT 105
March 1986

Creeping Death/ Am I Evil/ Blitzkrieg
Music For Nations 12KUT 112
Picture edition
Music For Nations P12KUT 112
November 1984

Reissued in gold vinyl
Music For Nations GV12KUT 112
Reissued in blue vinyl
Music For Nations BV12KUT 112
Reissued on CD
Music For Nations CD12 KUTT
January 1987

The $5.95 EP - Garage Days Revisited:
Helpless/ The Small Hours/ The Wait/ Crash Course In Brain Surgery/ Last Caress/ Green Hell
Vertigo METAL112
August 1987

Interview Picture Discs - 7" set
Baktabak BAKPAK 1015
August 1988

Harvester of Sorrow/ Breadfan/ The Prince
Vertigo METAL212
Also available on CD
Vertigo CD Metal CD2
September 1988

One/ Seek & Destroy (live) - 7"
Vertigo Metal5
April 1989

One/ For Whom The Bell Tolls (live)/ Welcome Home (Sanitarium) (live)
Vertigo METAL 512
Also available on CD
Vertigo CD METCD5
April 1989

One (album version)/ Seek & Destroy (live)
10" Picture disc
Vertigo METPD 510
April 1989

One (demo version)/ For Whom The Bell Tolls (live)/Creeping Death (live)
In Special Gatefold Sleeve
Vertigo METG 512
April 1989

The Good, The Bad & The Live: The Six And A Half Year 12" Collection. Includes all the above plus The Six And A Half Year Anniversary Live EP: Harvester of Sorrow (live)/ One (live)/ Breadfan (live)/ Last Caress (live)
Vertigo 88-788-1
May 1991

Enter Sandman/ Stone Cold Crazy - 7"
Vertigo METAL 7
August 1991

Enter Sandman/ Stone Cold Crazy/ Holier Than Thou/ Enter Sandman (demo version)
Vertigo METAL 712
August 1991

Enter Sandman/ Stone Cold Crazy/ Enter Sandman (demo version) - Boxed 12"
Vertigo METBX 712
Also available on CD
Vertigo CD METCD 7
August 1991

The Unforgiven/ Killing Time - 7"
Vertigo METAL 8
November 1991

The Unforgiven/ Killing Time/ So What/ The Unforgiven (demo version)
Vertigo METAL 812
Picture Disc
Vertigo METAP 812
Also available on CD
Vertigo CD METCD 8
November 1991

Nothing Else Matters/ Enter Sandman (live) - 7"
Vertigo METAL 10
April 1992

Nothing Else Matters/ Enter Sandman (live)/ Harvester of Sorrow (live)/ Nothing Else Matters (demo version)
Vertigo METAL 1012
Also available on CD
Vertigo METCD 10
April 1992

Enter Sandman (live)/ Stone Cold Crazy (live)/ Nothing Else Matters (live)
Vertigo METCD 10
April 1992

Wherever I May Roam/ Fade To Black - 7"
Vertigo METAL 9
October 1992

Wherever I May Roam/ Fade To Black/ Wherever I May Roam (demo version)
Vertigo METCD 9
October 1992

Wherever I May Roam/ Medley (live)/ Wherever I May Roam (demo version)
Vertigo METAL 912
October 1992

Wherever I May Roam/ Medley (live)
Digipak CD
Vertigo METCB 9
October 1992

Sad But True/ Nothing Else Matters
Vertigo METAL 11
February 1993

Sad But True/ Nothing Else Matters (elevator version)/ Creeping Death (live)/ Sad But True (demo version)
Vertigo METAL 1112
Also available on CD
Vertigo METCD 11
February 1993

Sad But True/Nothing Else Matters (live)/ Sad But True (live) CD
Vertigo METCH 11
February 1993

ALBUMS

KILL 'EM ALL
Hit The Lights/ The Four Horsemen/ Motorbreath/ Jump In The Fire/ (Anaesthesia) Pulling Teeth/ Whiplash/ Phantom Lord/ No Remorse/ Seek And Destroy/ Metal Militia
Music For Nations MFN7
Also available on CD
July 1983

Reissued as Picture Disc
Music For Nations MFN 7P
August 1986

RIDE THE LIGHTNING
Fight Fire With Fire/ Ride The Lightning/ For Whom The Bell Tolls/ Fade To Black/ Trapped Under Ice/ Escape/ Creeping Death/ The Call Of Ktulu
Music For Nations MFN27
Also available on CD
July 1984

Reissued as Picture Disc
Music For Nations MFN 27P
September 1986

MASTER OF PUPPETS
Battery/ Master of Puppets/ The Thing That Should Not Be/ Welcome Home (Sanitarium)/ Disposable Heroes/ Leper Messiah/ Orion/ Damage Inc
Music For Nations MFN60
Picture Disc
Music For Nations MFN 60P
Also available on CD
March 1986

Reissued as a double album
Music For Nations MFN60DM
December 1987

Chris Tetley Interviews Metallica
Music & Media CT 1008
September 1987

Interview Picture Disc
Baktabak BAK 2066
Also available on CD
September 1987

... AND JUSTICE FOR ALL
Blackened/ ... And Justice For All/ Eye Of The Beholder/ One/ The Shortest Straw/ Harvester of Sorrow/ The Frayed Ends Of Sanity/ To Live Is To Die/ Dyers Eve
Vertigo VERH61
Also available on CD
October 1988

The End Of The World As We Know It - Interview disc
Baktabak BAK 6011
January 1990

Interview Picture Disc
Baktabak BAK 2163
July 1990

METALLICA
Enter Sandman/Sad But True/Holier Than Thou/The Unforgiven/ Wherever I May Roam/ Don't Tread On Me/ Through The Never/ Nothing Else Matters/ Of Wolf And Man/ The God That Failed/ My Friend Of Misery/ The Struggle Within
Vertigo 5100221
August 1991

LIVE SHIT: BINGE AND PURGE
CD disc 1:
Enter Sandman/ Creeping Death/ Harvester of Sorrow/ (Welcome Home) Sanitarium/ Sad But True/ Of Wolf And Man/ The Unforgiven/ ... And Justice For All
CD Disc 2:
Through The Never/ For Whom The Bell Tolls/ Fade To Black/ Master Of Puppets/ Seek & Destroy/ Whiplash
CD Discs 3:
Nothing Else Matters/ Wherever I May Roam/ Am I Evil?/ Last Caress/ One/ Battery/ The Four Horsemen/ Motorbreath/ Stone Cold Crazy
Video 1:
Blackened/ For Whom The Bell Tolls/ (Welcome Home) Sanitarium/ Harvester Of Sorrow/ The Four Horsemen/ The Thing That Should Not Be/ Master Of Puppets/ Fade To Black/ Seek & Destroy/ ... And Justice For All/ One/ Creeping Death/ Battery/ Last Caress/ Am I Evil?/ Whiplash/ Breadfan
Video 2:
Enter Sandman/ Creeping Death/ Harvester Of Sorrow/ (Welcome Home) Sanitarium/ Sad But True/ Wherever I May Roam/ Through The Never/ The Unforgiven/ ... And Justice For All
Video 3:
The Four Horsemen/ For Whom The Bell Tolls/ Fade To Black/ Whiplash/ Master Of Puppets/ Seek & Destroy/ One/ Last Caress/ Am I Evil?/ Battery/ Stone Cold Crazy
Box Set contains 3 CDs, 3 videos, a 72-page booklet, a "snakepit" pass and stencil.
Cat. No. 518725-0
November 1993